A Note to Parents

DK READERS is a compelling program for beginning readers, designed in conjunction with leading literacy experts, including Dr. Linda Gambrell, Distinguished Professor of Education at Clemson University. Dr. Gambrell has served as President of the National Reading Conference, the College Reading Association, and the International Reading Association.

Beautiful illustrations and superb full-color photographs combine with engaging, easy-to-read stories to offer a fresh approach to each subject in the series. Each DK READER is guaranteed to capture a child's interest while developing his or her reading skills, general knowledge, and love of reading.

The five levels of DK READERS are aimed at different reading abilities, enabling you to choose the books that are exactly right for your child:

Pre-level 1: Learning to read
Level 1: Beginning to read
Level 2: Beginning to read alone
Level 3: Reading alone
Level 4: Proficient readers

The "normal" age at which a child begins to read can be anywhere from three to eight years old. Adult participation through the lower levels is very helpful for providing encouragement, discussing storylines, and sounding out unfamiliar words.

No matter which level you select, you can be sure that you are helping your child learn to read, then read to learn!

LONDON, NEW YORK, MUNICH,
MELBOURNE, and DELHI

Editor Shari Last
Managing Editor Laura Gilbert
Managing Art Editor Maxine Pedliham
Art Director Lisa Lanzarini
Publishing Manager Julie Ferris
Publishing Director Simon Beecroft
Pre-Production Producer Siu Yin Chan

DK India
Editor Rahul Ganguly
Senior Editor Garima Sharma
Assistant Art Editor Suzena Sengupta
Deputy Managing Art Editor Neha Ahuja
Pre-Production Manager Sunil Sharma

Lucasfilm
Executive Editor J. W. Rinzler
Art Director Troy Alders
Keeper of the Holocron Leland Chee
Director of Publishing Carol Roeder

Reading Consultant
Linda B. Gambrell, Ph.D.

First American Edition, 2014
14 15 16 10 9 8 7 6 5 4 3 2
002-187419-Mar/14

Published in the United States by DK Publishing
345 Hudson Street, New York, New York 10014

Published in Great Britain by Dorling Kindersley Limited

A catalog record for this book is available
from the Library of Congress.

ISBN: 978-1-4654-1682-7 (Paperback)
ISBN: 978-1-4654-1683-4 (Hardcover)

Color reproduction by Alta Image Ltd., UK
Printed and bound by
South China Printing Company Ltd., China

Discover more at
www.dk.com
www.starwars.com

Contents

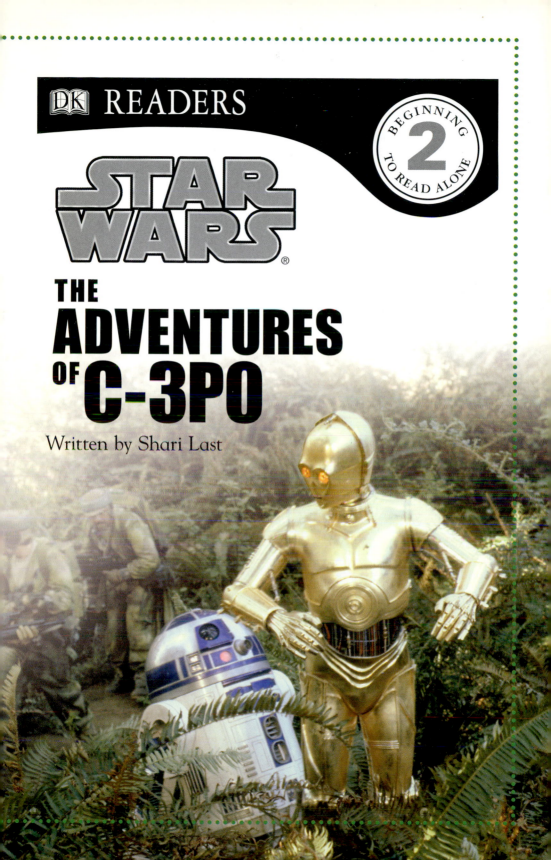

DK READERS

BEGINNING TO READ ALONE

2

STAR WARS®

THE ADVENTURES OF C-3PO

Written by Shari Last

Hello!

I am C-3PO.

How may I help you?

What's that?

You don't want my help?

You want to hear
about my adventures?
Well, that is a strange request.

But, of course, I am
programmed to be of service.
Now, where shall I begin?

Master Ani

I was built on the
planet Tatooine by
a young slave boy
named Anakin
Skywalker.

I called him "Master Ani."
He wanted to build a droid
helper for his mother.

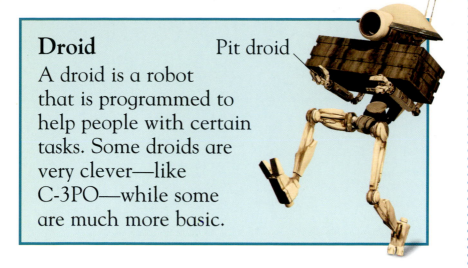

Droid   Pit droid

A droid is a robot that is programmed to help people with certain tasks. Some droids are very clever—like C-3PO—while some are much more basic.

Of course, I am much smarter than a regular droid. I can speak more than six million languages.

But I still helped Master Ani and his mother because I was a service droid and I always obeyed my master.

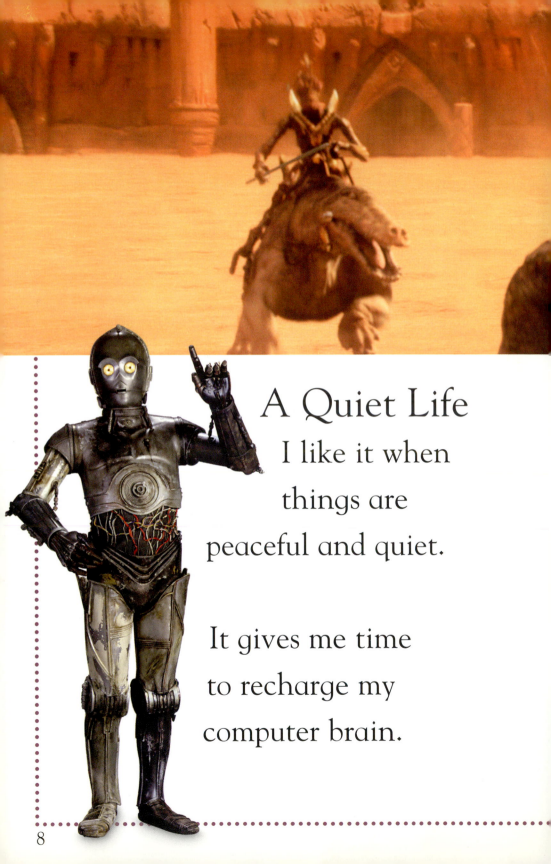

A Quiet Life

I like it when
things are
peaceful and quiet.

It gives me time
to recharge my
computer brain.

I am programmed to help
people communicate.
I am not built for battle.

But everything changed when
Master Ani grew older and
became a Jedi Knight. I traveled
with him to faraway planets and
joined him on many adventures!

Droid Mix-up

Once, Master Anakin and I
went to the planet Geonosis
where we discovered a secret
droid factory.

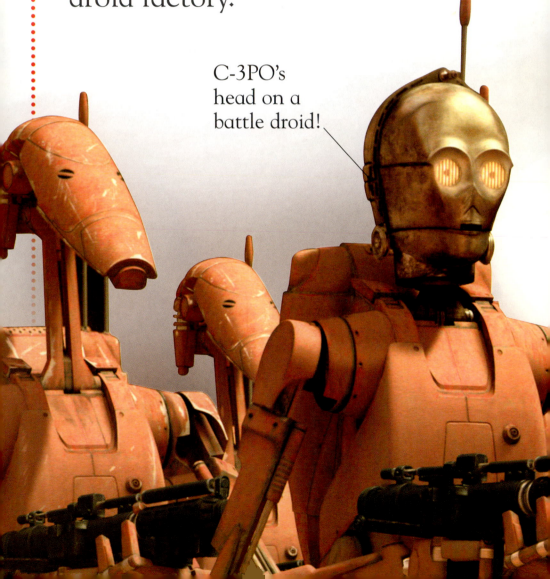

C-3PO's
head on a
battle droid!

Droid factory
There are many droid factories on Geonosis. In them, huge machines build thousands of battle droids.

Unfortunately, I fell into the factory and became all mixed up with a dangerous battle droid.

I was so distressed when I found myself right in the middle of a scary battle.

Cheeky Best Friend

R2-D2 is a cheeky little astromech droid.

We met on Tatooine and have been best friends ever since.

R2-D2 is very brave and clever, but he often likes to be rude and silly!

Astromech droids
Astromech droids, such as R2-D2, are small and clever droids. They fix broken starships and help with navigation.

Don't worry, I always tell him what to do.

And he listens to me… sometimes.

Oh No… Jawas!

One of the things I hate
most is getting lost.
I like to feel safe.

So you can
imagine how
upset I was when
R2-D2 and I
were captured
by a group of
horrible Jawas.

Jawas live in the deserts of
Tatooine and sell scrap metal.

First of all, I am not scrap metal.
Secondly, their massive
sandcrawler vehicle
was very dirty!

Jawas
Jawas are small, scary
creatures with glowing
yellow eyes. They will sell
anything they find, so
don't get too close!

A Friendly Droid

I have made lots of new
friends on my adventures.

Jedi Knight Luke Skywalker
bought me from the Jawas.
He is my new master now,
but he is also my friend.

Princess Leia

Chewbacca

Luke's sister is Princess Leia.
She goes on secret missions to
make the galaxy a safer place.

Han Solo is a pilot.
His best friend, Chewbacca,
is a tall, hairy Wookiee.

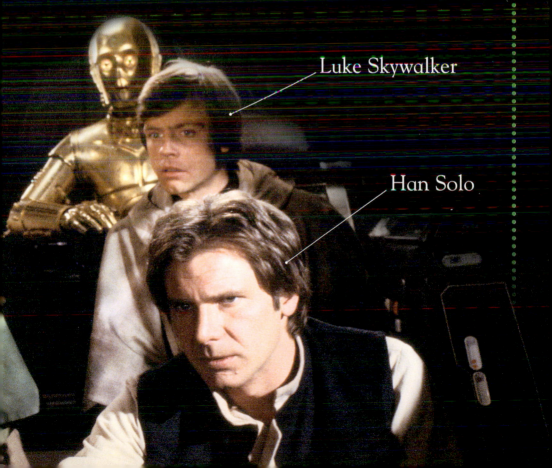

Luke Skywalker

Han Solo

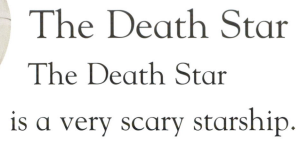

The Death Star

The Death Star
is a very scary starship.
But Master Luke is not
afraid of anything. We went
to the Death Star to rescue a
prisoner, Princess Leia.

But my friends Leia, Han,
and Luke got trapped in a
garbage masher, which was
about to squash them!

I am proud to tell you
that I saved them.
I told R2-D2 to turn off the
garbage masher just in time.
What a close call!

Blown to Bits

One of my worst adventures
was on Cloud City.
I walked into the wrong room—
and was blown to bits!
It was very upsetting.

Luckily, my friend Chewbacca
picked up all my pieces.
He carried me around
in a backpack until he
had time to mend me.
Even though he made a few
mistakes when putting me back
together, I was very grateful.

Working for Jabba

Jabba the Hutt is a big, slimy, disgusting creature!
He loves capturing and bothering innocent people.

He captured me once and forced me to be his translator. I hated it!

When I worked for Jabba, I was treated with no respect— even by his pet, Salacious Crumb!

I was very pleased when Master Luke defeated Jabba and rescued me.

Salacious Crumb
This is Jabba's favorite pet. He must make Jabba laugh at least once a day or he will be in big trouble.

Ewok Admirers

I often think that none of my friends truly appreciate how wonderful and special I am. The Ewoks do, though.

Ewoks are small, tough creatures who live on the forest moon of Endor.

The Ewoks were fascinated by my shiny gold body. They listened to everything I said, and they helped my friends and me on our mission.

To the Rescue!

Once, R2-D2 and I were
hiding in the forest of Endor
when a group of stormtroopers
captured our friends.

I wanted to help my friends,
so I shouted to the stormtroopers
and they came chasing after me.

But I tricked them!
When they came
near, an army of
Ewoks jumped out
of the trees and
helped us defeat
the stormtroopers.
Hooray!

Stormtroopers
Stormtroopers are soldiers
who work for an evil Empire.
They wear white armor and
carry deadly blasters.

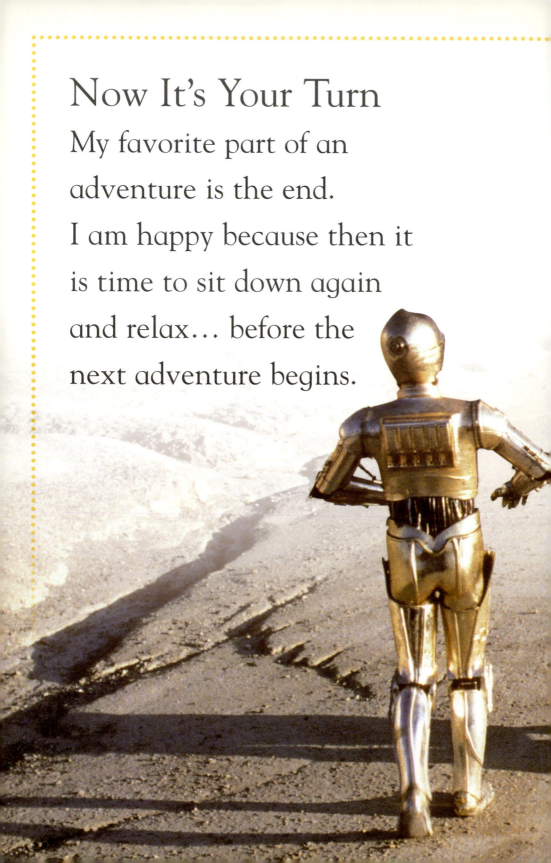

Now It's Your Turn

My favorite part of an
adventure is the end.
I am happy because then it
is time to sit down again
and relax… before the
next adventure begins.

But remember, you don't have to fly in starships or travel around the galaxy to have amazing adventures.

You can go on an exciting adventure wherever you are!

Quiz

1. On which planet are the droid factories?

2. Who is C-3PO's best friend?

3. What creatures sell scrap metal on Tatooine?

4. Where was Princess Leia held prisoner?

5.Who is Jabba the Hutt's pet?

Answers: 1. Geonosis 2. R2-D2 3. Jawas 4. On the Death Star 5. Salacious Crumb

Index

Here are some other DK Readers you might enjoy.

Level 2

LEGO® *Star Wars*: Attack of the Clones
Meet evil Count Dooku! Can the Republic's clone troopers defeat the Sith's droid army?

***Star Wars*: Bounty Hunters for Hire**
Who are the mysterious and dangerous bounty hunters? Learn all their scary secrets.

***Star Wars*: Chewbacca and the Wookiee Warriors**
Chewbacca battles for his life with the help of the Jedi and his ferocious Wookiee warriors!

Level 3

LEGO® *Star Wars*: Revenge of the Sith
The Jedi must save the galaxy from the Sith! Will Anakin fall to the dark side?

***Star Wars*: The Legendary Yoda**
Yoda is a famous and wise Jedi. Learn all about his legendary battles and how he uses the Force.

***Star Wars*: Obi-Wan Kenobi, Jedi Knight**
Meet Obi-Wan Kenobi! Learn all about his journey to become a legendary Jedi Master.